Meditations From Downtown

A Counselor's Reflections on Life

Ralph F. Ranieri

LIGUORI PUBLICATIONS

One Liguori Drive
Liguori, Missouri 63057-9999
(314) 464-2500

Imprimi Potest:
James Shea, C.SS.R.
Provincial, St. Louis Province
The Redemptorists

Imprimatur:
Most Rev. Edward J. O'Donnell, D.D., V.G.
Auxiliary Bishop
Archdiocese of St. Louis

ISBN 0-89243-326-4
Library of Congress Catalog Card Number: 90-61149

CONTENTS

1

PRAYING FOR THINGS

When I was in my teens, attending a Catholic high school, I used to "pray for things" — mainly to win basketball games and pass exams.

When I was in my twenties, I stopped "praying for things." There were no more exams to pass or games to win, and I felt I could do everything myself anyhow.

When I was in my thirties, I still didn't "pray for things." By then I was having some trouble doing a few things, but I figured that with my intelligence and experience I could eventually work things out. No need to panic or pray, I thought.

Now I'm in my forties, and I pray for everything. In the last decade I've realized that I'll never be smart enough or experienced enough to handle all the unseen turns of life. I need all the help I can get.

I used to consider the prayer of petition a lower form of prayer. But now I realize that it is the prayer of wise men and women — those who have come to grips with their own limits and the need for God's grace.

Another reason I had trouble in the past with prayers of petition is that I thought God wanted us to solve all our own problems. Don't ask me how I ever came up with that idea, but a lot of Christians share it. They imagine that God watches from the wings while we have to go it alone for the most part.

But without denying my own responsibilities, I'm sure now that God wants us to pray for things. In the gospels he tells us to ask and we will receive. If we have faith, he says in another place, we can move mountains. As active and responsible as some of the saints were, they all prayed for their own needs and the needs of the people they served. Praying for things is an acceptable way of relating to our loving Father.

Where does our responsibility stop and God's providence take over? Why don't we get all our prayers answered? I don't know. I've stopped trying to answer those questions. Sometimes there are no answers. That's what faith is for.

I have decided that I'll do my best. I'll continue to pray for things; but I'll leave how, when, where — and if — he intervenes up to God.

I've noticed that when I pray for things, I feel sincere and unselfish, not at all as if I'm performing a second-rate form of prayer. When I pray for things, I'm praying from the heart because I sincerely need many things, and I know many people in need.

I once heard a preacher call prayer the "cry of the heart." My heart cries out for many things I need to get along in life, for things I hold dear and precious. If I try to deny these needs and just pray prayers of praise, if I ask God for nothing and try to be unselfish, my heart isn't always in it. Sometimes my heart is bound up with my needs.

When I'm alone with God, asking his assistance because I can't get through to my son, I feel anything but superficial. This is a prayer of petition, but it is for something that is vitally important to me. It is a part of what my life is all about.

I could pray vaguely, telling God that he is everything in my life. But when I come alone to him and ask him to give me the grace to salvage a major part of my life, I am not only telling God that he is everything, I am experiencing him as everything. I am experiencing him as my hope — at times my only hope.

A man lying in a hospital bed told about his experience as he waited for the results of a biopsy. "I had never prayed for myself," he said. "I didn't want to turn God into a wishing well. But I did pray for myself this week, and I don't think I ever encountered God in such a real way before. When you are literally asking God to let you live, you get a real sense that you are talking to a powerful person. That's when you realize just how dependent you are on him in life and in death. Even though I was praying for myself, it was the closest moments I had ever felt to God."

Praying for things is not secondary prayer. It is a powerful form of prayer in which we recognize that we are limited children and God is our infinite, loving Father.

2

BEING OVERLOOKED

It was just another business meeting — or so I thought. I usually enjoyed the coffee and jokes and good wishes of friends that preceded these meetings. But mostly I was flattered by the attention my colleagues paid to my ideas.

But something was different about this meeting. Many of the faces were not familiar, and the people I recognized didn't seem to recognize me. My attempts at humor fell flat. Much of our confidence comes from others, no matter how mature we like to think we are; conversely, much of our confidence can be taken away by others.

When it was my turn to speak, I brought out my carefully prepared notes on what I thought was an important issue. But instead of giving me their rapt attention, my audience leafed through handouts, doodled, and gazed out the window as I spoke. Worse yet, when I finished talking, the responses were directed to a different subject from the one I had addressed.

I wasn't just rejected; I was unnoticed. What I had to say did not warrant a response. The little snubs — the ones no one else notices — are often the most painful. Little snubs leave us alone, with no one to blame and no one to apologize to us.

It always seemed to me that humility was reserved for those grand moments in life. Saint Francis showed his humility by helping a leper. Mother Teresa shows hers by holding a dying man. But most of us can't wait for the grand moments to be humble. We need humility to cope with the constant snubs and oversights of life. Humility is something that has to be part and parcel of our character if we are to be truly Christian or, for that matter, even socially acceptable.

A business meeting is just one setting where we can find ourselves completely overlooked. Just look at some other areas of everyday life in which humility would help, not only on a spiritual level but a practical one as well. Often our children fail to realize how much we do for them. At times our spouses may not pay attention to us, even when we ask for it. Busy friends may ignore or forget us temporarily. Then there are all those people who fail to thank us, write to us, or answer our calls.

People who are short on humility sometimes strike back. "How dare they ignore me!" they say to themselves. Then they may make a sharp comment or try to find some way of returning the hurt in kind. The result is tension at work, power struggles with the kids, and arguments with spouses or friends. This hardly creates an atmosphere of Christian community or even a comfortable living environment.

If we had a little humility, we would be less likely to want everything while feeling we deserve nothing. On the other hand, we would recognize that other people are forgetful, insensitive at times, often preoccupied, and occasionally self-centered. We could feel confident about what we have to say and what we stand for, even when others fail to pat us on the back or pay rapt attention to our words.

We deserve good treatment, but we can't expect preferential treatment as a rule. If we get it, we're fortunate. We have to realize that being overlooked at times is part of life, not an injustice.

During his earthly life, Jesus was often overlooked. For thirty years no one knew he was anything more than a village carpenter. During his public life, some people still couldn't see him as anything more than the son of Joseph the carpenter. Yet Jesus never complained about the lack of attention. He accepted this lack as something he had to work with.

Elizabeth Ann Seton, a beautiful and prominent socialite, nursed her dying husband in a foreign country, without the benefit of the medical care and preferential treatment she would have enjoyed in Baltimore. Even though she was used to social prestige and the company of important people such as George Washington, she didn't consider the lack of attention an injustice. Rather, she endured it and set herself to the task at hand.

Humility helps us accept that being overlooked is a normal, natural, everyday part of life. We don't need a monastery to find opportunities for humility; we can find ample opportunities right here, downtown.

3

DOING ROUTINE STUFF

Every day I get up on the same side of the bed. I pour coffee from the same pot. I step into the same shower and search the same house for my seven-year-old's same pair of sneakers. And that's only the beginning of my routine. I drive the same route to work and ride the same elevator to the same office to do the same thing.

In the midst of all this routine, I fantasize about doing the "real stuff" that the saints do. In my fantasy I break out of my boring routine and perform exciting tasks. I'm Mother Teresa's right-hand man, saving people on the streets of Calcutta. Or I'm negotiating a peace settlement in some war-torn corner of the world. Here's one of my favorites: I come up with a plan to feed the hungry, and all the world leaders go along with it.

But while I'm mentally out in space saving an imaginary world, the real world is passing unnoticed right in front of me. There's a phone call to be returned. There's a student who needs a letter of recommendation. There's a meeting to attend. A child needs help with a math problem.

These are not very dramatic calls to duty, but they are real. They are the only places at this point where I can show the love of God. It makes no difference to God whether the task is dramatic or routine, whether it is high profile or goes unnoticed, as long as it is done with love.

Dreaming is fine, but I must be careful that I don't become an "apostolic snob," thinking that certain types of work are beneath me. This would only lead me to keep dreaming of the ideal work and lead me further away from the real work.

Sigmund Freud didn't give spiritual advice, but we can translate his basic premise into sound spiritual counsel. In short, Freud believed that neurotics spend more time in fantasy than reality. Spiritually translated, we can say that many good Christians miss their chance at sanctity because they spend more time dreaming about what they could do rather than getting down and doing what they can do.

There's gold in our routines. That's where we will become holy, by faithfully carrying out the tasks that lie before us. Most of us are not like Lincoln, Churchill, Ghandi, or Joan of Arc. We don't live on the cutting edge of history. We occasionally have peak moments, but most of our time is spent in routine. If we are to live close to Jesus, we must do so within the context of our routines.

Jesus spent thirty years living the routine of a village carpenter. There must have been many routine days in his public life as he walked from town to town, ate meals, and talked with his disciples.

Even the saints, who seem at times to have lived very dramatic lives, often led quite ordinary, routine ones. Saint John Bosco saved hundreds of young boys from the streets of Turin. That sounds dramatic when you read an account condensed into three or four pages. But what could be more routine than living every day, year after year, in a house full of poorly mannered boys? Some of his greatest acts of sanctity might have occurred in the course of his routine as he listened to this boy or encouraged that boy, while being tired or preoccupied himself.

If we are sensitive, we can find many opportunities for genuine Christian action in our routine. In one day a mother might skip breakfast to coax her school-phobic son to the bus stop; drive four miles out of her way to pick up a coworker with car trouble; listen patiently while another coworker talks about financial problems; visit a friend who has had surgery; break up one fight between the neighborhood kids and two between her own; help with twenty math problems, forty spelling words, and fifteen social studies questions; answer a total of seventeen phone calls; and go to a Marriage Encounter meeting.

That's routine. But it's also sanctity if it is done with love day after day. Going to school, teaching the same class, sitting in the same office, talking with the same coworkers, helping the same people, answering the phone, attending meetings, cooking meals, slowing down to talk to a person in need — all are paths to holiness.

It is hard to make our routines holy. We've been doing them for so long they seem anything but sacred. That's why we have to pray. We'd be much closer to Jesus if we prayed daily for the grace to go through our routines with genuine love.

4

FILLING THE GAP

Today the word *yuppie* has become almost synonymous with greed. When social commentators and comedians use the word, they are usually referring to young people who are compulsive consumers with materialistic values.

It is true that many people today are materialistic. They may be too concerned about their cars, homes, VCRs, clubs, and pastimes. They may be so bent on acquiring money and material things that they forget Christians are supposed to be concerned about others.

As Christians we all know how devastating greed can be. We've heard all kinds of stories about money not being everything. Money, we've been told, is the root of all evil. But we miss the point about greed if we look at it only in terms of money and material possessions. Greed is the inordinate desire to have more than we need. And this can refer to more than just material things.

If we want to eradicate greed in our lives, we have to eradicate it at its root. Greed goes beyond material things. We can be greedy about

- the amount of attention we want from our spouses,
- the amount of time we want alone,
- the amount of time we want for hobbies,
- the amount of time we spend on TV,
- the amount of respect we want from our children,
- the amount of praise we want from our friends,
- the amount of weight we want to lose,
- the amount of time we want to spend on our work,
- even the amount of time we want for quiet prayer.

An inordinate desire to have more than we need in any area of life is detrimental to our relationships with God and the people we love. If we want to overcome our greed for material things, we can't simply transfer it to greed for spiritual things. We have to go to the roots of our greed and replace it with something else.

A friend I hadn't seen in fifteen years, a man with a severe disability, visited my home recently. In those fifteen years this man had started an organization for the handicapped and turned it into a strong and powerful influence in his community. He had organized a board of directors from the community. As executive director of the board, he was reaching people of all ages, helping them to realize that they could get out and live.

In the course of our conversation, I used the phrase "job security" in reference to my work, and my friend broke out in laughter.

"Job security?" he said. "What job security?"

It immediately dawned on me how little job security this man must have had throughout his life, not to mention how little job security he had when he started his organization. I felt a pang of guilt.

Then he said to me, "Faith, man. It takes faith, not job security, to do anything."

If we want to cut out greed at its root — whether it is greed for money, material things, or job security or the spiritual greed of the self-righteous — what we have to do is replace it with faith.

Perhaps if we had more faith, we would be less demanding. Maybe if we had more faith, we wouldn't be constantly craving the perfect response from everyone in our lives. People who are greedy for love make constant demands on others. This usually leaves all concerned chronically dissatisfied.

Sure there is a gap in our lives. Of course we feel like there is something missing. But if we don't have faith filling this gap, we will be doomed to trying to fill it up with other things. The frenetic pace at which we keep trying to fill the gap is what makes us feel and sometimes appear greedy.

That's why the spiritual life is so important. It fills in the gap between the limits of reality and the perfection we all yearn for. Saint Augustine sought to fill the gap in his life through a greedy search for physical pleasure and intellectual prominence. When that didn't work, he found true peace in faith, confessing that our hearts "will know no rest until they rest in you."

For complete fullness in life, we must turn to God. Faith roots out greed.

5

FINDING YOUR BALANCE

Everyone wants to lose weight and be trim. A writer jokingly said he could write a bestseller every time if he just included the words "how to lose weight" in the title.

Yet there is an age-old way to lose weight and maintain the loss. It is safe and healthy, and it is thousands of years old. Although their main goal wasn't weight loss, Aristotle and the wisdom writers of the Old Testament recommended this method. And it has been part of the Christian tradition for centuries.

The plan is temperance. Practicing temperance means never eating or drinking more than you need. Enjoy your food all you want, but eat it in moderate portions. Actually, temperance helps you enjoy your food more. Believe it or not, temperance is not part of the latest fad diet. Temperance is a virtue that leads us closer to God.

If you don't believe that temperance leads you closer to God, have you ever tried to pray after stuffing yourself at an all-you-can-eat buffet or after three martinis? It is hard to make yourself comfortable in those circumstances, let alone pray.

Of course the problem of obesity is more complex than that. Many people, due to the chemical makeup of their bodies, are overweight even though they eat relatively small amounts of food. Others suffer from eating disorders that make successful weight loss a matter for professional counseling.

Still, the practice of temperance is within everyone's capability and has a direct bearing on our health and self-concept. Temperance makes us better able to give ourselves to others. It is difficult to give our attention to those who are with us when we are worried about what or how much we will get to eat. When we are overloaded with food, it is difficult to get up and visit the sick or write a letter to a friend. We prefer to rest.

The wisdom writer Sirach has some descriptive words about overeating:

> Be not drawn after every enjoyment,
> neither become a glutton for choice foods,
> For sickness comes with overeating,
> and gluttony brings on biliousness.
>
> (Sirach 37:28-29)

Temperance is not simply an attitude toward food and drink, however; it is an attitude toward life. To be moderate with food and drink, we have to be moderate in all areas of life.

"I prayed for the virtue of temperance," an overweight woman said, "then it hit me: I had gone overboard in many areas of life. Not only did I eat too much, I wasn't getting any exercise. I was spending too much money and was too involved outside the home. The insight I received from my prayer was that I should bring moderation into my whole life."

So in an attempt to practice temperance, this woman began to rise half an hour earlier in the morning and use that time for walking and praying. Instead of shopping and being overinvolved outside the home, she relaxed with her family. With a more moderate pace, she prepared better meals in a slower manner. At meal times she began to enjoy both her food and her family more. Just moving slower and being more relaxed helped her eat less. Such a change helped her to move closer to God and her family.

Temperance has a far-reaching effect because it is one of those virtues that sets the stage for other positive changes in our lives. So examine your life to see what you can do to put more balance into it. If your life is weighted too far in one direction, then it is a sign that perhaps you have room to make some adjustments and be a bit more temperate.

Throughout the centuries holy men and women have struggled to find a balance between using food wisely and abusing it. They struggled to find a balance between rest and work, poverty and materialism, prayer and service, family and community.

To balance our lives is to exercise the virtue of temperance. It is a virtue worth struggling for because it has such far-reaching effects, both spiritual and physical.

6

LOOKING GOOD

We spend a great deal of money in this country in pursuit of looking good. The amount of money spent each year on clothes and cosmetics alone is staggering. A few years ago more money was spent on eye makeup than on eye research. The weight loss industry is another booming business today. We diet and exercise not only for our health but to also look good.

If only we spent as much time and energy working on what goes on inside of us as we do on the outside, there would be a major change in all of us.

As Christians we know that Jesus looks at hearts, not faces, fashions, and figures. As Christians we know that Jesus is more concerned with the love we have inside us than with our superficial appearance. Because of our humanity — and the value society places on surface beauty — we continue to spend our time, our energy, and our money on trying to look good.

It's bad enough when we are preoccupied with our own attractiveness. But subtle problems can arise when we are overly concerned with the way other people look. We often choose our public officials by the appearance they make on a thirty-second TV spot. We spend less and less time, it seems, looking inside our leaders for long-lasting qualities such as honesty, dedication, and competence.

We gravitate to friends, not only friends of the opposite sex but all friends, who make a nice appearance. We just presume that people who look good *are* good. This mistaken attitude leads to major problems, not only for children and adolescents but for adults as well. Yet the people who turn out to be our best friends may not necessarily be the ones who look the best.

The danger for serious Christians in all this is that too much emphasis on looking good can make us superficial. Too much concern for our appearance and that of our friends eventually ends up trivializing our own self-worth and the worth of our relationships.

Jesus was pretty emphatic about the unimportance of externals. It isn't washing your hands that is important, he tells us, but what is in your heart. It isn't the type of clothes you wear or the trappings of authority that dangle from you like ornaments but what's in your heart.

It's too bad we can't try to outdo one another, as Saint Paul says, by doing good rather than trying to outdo others by looking good. It's too bad we don't practice patience so we may bear with one another with as much enthusiasm as we give to sit-ups and push-ups in order to appear attractive to one another. It's too bad that cheering up a sick friend doesn't excite us as much as buying a new outfit.

Of course good health is important. Our bodies are gifts, and the way we show our appreciation for a gift is to take care of it. And certainly looking good is important. Being clean and neat and as attractive as we can is the charitable thing to do. But it's not the most important thing. What is in our hearts is most important. The desire to reach out to one another, sharing love and building a peaceful community, is what really counts.

If we stop and think about it, the qualities on the inside are the ones that last, not the physical features on the outside. No matter how good we may look, we're going to lose a little bit of that as time goes by. But inner qualities do not fade. In fact they grow. Love, peace, and a desire to share with others get stronger with age.

The secret to happiness, both on this earth and in everlasting life, is to make sure our first concern is with the inside, then we can do what needs to be done for the outside.

7

BEING ADEQUATE

Lord, deliver me from the worst fate of all — that of being judged inadequate.

Our forefathers may have dreaded the abominable plague that could ravage them and their families. But today we dread — almost with equal terror — being judged inadequate.

We fear that we will be inadequate as parents or spouses. Consequently, we relentlessly seek out ways to be better in every way. And all the time we are restless, berating ourselves for our lack of perfection. If we have a problem in our marriage or meet with opposition from the children, we are the first to think of ourselves as woefully inadequate.

We fear that we will be inadequate as lovers. The number of self-help books on the subject proves just how much we fear this one. We fear that we will be inadequate as workers. So we run at a frenetic pace, not only during busy times but all the time. We just can't seem to do enough to squelch the fear of inadequacy.

And when we aren't worrying about whether or not we are adequate, we worry about the adequacy of our children. Are they toilet-trained as quickly as the other kids in their play group? Are they reading as soon as the other four-year-olds? Are they popular? Will they be accepted by the "right" college? Will they meet the right person, have the right kind of children so that we all can live adequately ever after?

We will never rest, it seems, until we are assured that we and our children are and will continue to be adequate. This frame of mind certainly isn't the way to peace; it is the way to worry, anxiety, and frustration. It leads away from God and others.

The more active saints have always impressed me. They did a great deal of work in the world, living lives of high visibility. Everybody could see their mistakes as well as their accomplishments. Yet they never seemed concerned with how they looked. Whether others judged them adequate or inadequate never seemed to be their main concern. Perhaps this added to their effectiveness.

Yet from a strictly human, organizational point of view, these people accomplished amazing things. They founded religious orders, which meant dealing with red tape and sometimes temperamental people who disagreed with them. They organized mass relief for the needy. They founded schools, shelters, and institutions.

Through it all, these saints never worried about society's report card. Being adequate or inadequate didn't matter to them. What mattered was their intentions, their love, and God's will.

Even when the saints were not successful, they didn't worry about their adequacy. As Lord Chancellor of England under Henry VIII, Saint Thomas More's duties kept him away from his wife and children. He felt the loss when his commitment to the king kept him away from his daughter's sixteenth birthday celebration. Yet he continued to juggle his life, trying to keep his family, his faith, his job, and his head. Since he did his best, he felt right with God and didn't worry about his adequacy.

Most of us are in the same position today. As husbands and wives, mothers and fathers, we struggle to keep everything going in our complex lives. We do all we can at work and try to give our remaining strength to family. If we find a few minutes, we pray and remind our children to pray. In little ways we do what we can to keep values alive while the world bombards our lives and homes. Now after doing all that, we deserve a medal. We don't deserve to sit in judgment of ourselves; we don't need others to sit in judgment of us, deciding whether or not we are adequate.

Adequacy was never the issue for Jesus. What counted most with him was intention. The widow's intention counted for more than what she gave. The adultress' intention to "sin no more" counted for more than what she did. Peter's intention counted for more than what he said.

It is our intention that counts too. We may have trouble on the job. We may have difficulty with the children. We may not be able to communicate as well as we would like with our spouses. But what counts is our intention. Do we love? Do we try? Do we want to do God's will?

If we can answer yes, then in God's eyes we are well beyond what the world calls adequate.

8

BEING A SUCCESS

Success means different things to different people. But for most people success means accomplishing the task they set out to do. This kind of success is well defined in our society. Did he get promoted? If he did, he must have done the task he set out to do. Therefore, he must be successful. Did she get a raise? Then she must have done the task she set out to do. So she too must be successful. They just got a bigger house. Then there is no doubt that they must be successful.

And so it goes. So-and-so is featured in the local paper; that must mean So-and-So is successful. Another person wins an award or is named teacher, parent, social worker, or salesperson of the year. That too must be a sign of success.

If that is the kind of success we are striving for, we are way off the mark as Christians. Sure, Christians are supposed to use their talents to the best of their ability. And if that makes them better salespersons, nurses, managers, or receptionists — fine. But the final trappings of success aren't that important.

Remember, Jesus became quite irritated with the Pharisees' desire to look successful by wearing the right clothes, having the right titles, and sitting in the right places. Jesus did not place the same value as the Pharisees on the external manifestations of success. In Jesus' eyes people like the Good Samaritan, who went out of his way to help another, was a successful person. The father of the Prodigal Son was another successful person in Jesus' way of thinking. He waited and waited for his son. Then when he saw him coming, he ran down the road to meet him.

Jesus asked that we not bother chasing the external symbols of success. He asked us to wash our faces when we fast and to go into our rooms when we pray so we could avoid receiving honors for our actions. So for the Christian, fidelity to God's law of love — not success — is the important thing. Someone once asked Mother Teresa if she worried about all her responsibilities. She replied, "God has not called me to be successful but faithful."

If there ever was a saint who was more concerned with faithfulness than success, it was Joseph, the foster father of Jesus and the husband of Mary. The usual trappings of success were absent in his life. He received no honors and had no titles. He worked at a trade that was honorable but not prestigious. He lived simply, without the material possessions that signify success. He even lacks the minimal criterion for success today, a high profile. Saint Joseph is continuously overlooked and sometimes even forgotten.

He lacked the symbols of worldly success, but Joseph was faithful. He was always there, quietly deciding to go ahead with his intention to wed Mary, even though she was with child. He was there protecting his family as they traveled during a time when travel was dangerous. He was there providing for them by plying his trade as a carpenter.

He was there, time after time. When Mary or the young Jesus looked up, he was there. He was there in the good times in Nazareth. He was there in the bad times when he was confused and couldn't understand. Certainly many men of his day received greater honors, had higher positions and grander titles, yet accomplished nothing of lasting value. Joseph's contribution was his faithfulness.

If faithfulness means anything today, it means being there — day after day, year after year. It means being there to celebrate the joys and grieve for the sorrows. It means being there when we are not receiving the love we crave, the respect we deserve, or the fulfillment we want.

Like Joseph, the faithful person is there in the home, on the job, in a friendship, committed to the problem son or daughter. Faithful people may not always know what to do. But as they pray and look for the answers, they are there; and they stay there because they are faithful.

That's faithfulness. That's the virtue that ultimately makes for success but is more important than the success itself. It is a simple yet powerful virtue with the potential to affect even our children's children.

What the Church and society need today are not more successful people who take up media space and get promotions and raises, but more people who are willing to be there where they are needed.

9

LAUGHING IT OFF

A good sense of humor is more than just the ability to deliver a well-timed punch line. A sense of humor may have nothing at all to do with making other people laugh or with being the life of the party.

A good sense of humor is the ability to see the human side of life. People with a sense of humor see what is laughable about daily life. They recognize the predictable and universal in the human struggle.

Because they see the humanness in life and know our failures and foibles are predictable, they do not take themselves too seriously. Now I don't mean they have no concern for their good name or that they consider themselves foolish, but they don't take failures and shortcomings to mean more than just what they are — human problems.

Watch a good comedy film or TV show and notice how it makes fun of a human side of life we can all identify with. It might portray characters afraid to spend the night in a dark old mansion. We can all identify with a situation like that, for there is a certain amount of fear in all of us. An episode of a situation comedy may derive humor from a parent's attempts to communicate with a teenager. Every parent has been through this and can laugh at these attempts. Another show may depict a good-hearted person who is unable to say no to a friend for fear of hurting the friend's feelings. Many of us have been in this position too, and we can laugh at that.

But a true Christian sense of humor involves not only the ability to laugh at others in human situations but to laugh at ourselves as well. We don't have to laugh out loud, nor do we have to make fun of ourselves in the presence of others. But instead of losing our self-esteem when we become involved in a very human situation, we have to be able to laugh at ourselves and try again.

Sometimes we set our goals too high and fail to reach them. We have to be able to laugh at ourselves for wanting to be more than we can be at times. We can try again, but someone with a true sense of humor won't take failure as if it were too terribly important.

Pope John XXIII was probably one of the most lovable personalities in the sixties. He was loved because his humanness showed. He wasn't afraid of how he appeared to others. He was short and overweight, and he had not held traditionally prestigious positions prior to becoming pope. Furthermore, he was generally thought of as only an interim pope.

None of this seemed to bother Pope John, though. He definitely did not take himself too seriously. He recognized what was imperfect about himself. He could laugh at his own foibles. Yet he did so without losing any respect for himself or the lofty office he held.

According to one story, Pope John called an adviser one day and said, "I'd like to have an Ecumenical Council."

The adviser was stunned. "That would take five years to prepare," he gasped.

"Fine," the Pope answered. "We will have it in one year." Obviously, the possibility of failing did not freeze this pope with fear. If he had lacked a sense of humor or worried unduly about tarnishing his image, he would have played it safe and never tried to have a Council.

But just as a sense of humor keeps us from fearing failure, it can also keep us from taking our successes to mean that we are more than we really are. If we succeed, we have to thank God, be proud of ourselves, and remember that earthly glory is fleeting. At best, life is temporary. Too often our success will yield only temporary rewards because it will be short-lived in people's memories. To recognize this fact is not to take the negative view. To be able to laugh at our overinflated sense of success is a sign of a healthy sense of humor.

People who see their success as proof that they are better than others often become overbearing and hard to live with. They are also the ones who fall the farthest when they encounter setbacks. Humor makes us humble. It enables us to live more realistically with our neighbor and ourselves. But most of all when we look at our humanness with good humor, we are in the best position for turning to God.

10

LETTING GO

Gaining, striving, and acquiring don't cause me too many problems. I'm competitive, I can assert myself when necessary, and I have a fair amount of ambition. But in this I'm no different from many other people I know whose main problems are not in these areas. There is always room for improvement; but by and large, American Christians have a history of building churches and schools, spreading the faith, and rising to prominence in business, education, and other fields.

Most of our problems do not come from what we can't get. The majority of our problems — especially in midlife — come from what we can't let go of. Our depressions stem from the guilt we can't let go of. Our restlessness stems from the anger we can't release. Our irritations come from the hurts we can't let go of and forgive. Our poor self-images come from the mistakes we insist upon replaying in our minds rather than letting go of.

It goes on and on. We struggle with our children because we can't let go of them. We argue with our spouses because we can't let go of them and let them be themselves. We fight with our bodies because we can't let go of our youth and accept the aging process. We grieve for prolonged periods of time because we can't emotionally let go of a deceased loved one.

The problem is spiritual as well as emotional. Prayer is difficult for those who can't let go of their thoughts and their need to control everything, including God. It's hard to experience the love of God if we can't let go of the haunting image of God as a taskmaster who measures every step we take and never forgets those "old sins."

It's almost impossible to serve others the way we would serve Jesus if we can't let go of our own guilt, annoyances, or need to have others respond as we want them to respond.

Jesus is the perfect model of a person who let go. Even though he was God, he let go and became human. As a human he let go of his life. Throughout his human life, while he worked energetically to spread the kingdom, he was always ready to let go. He never coerced his disciples. He let go of them. He let them be themselves. How tempted would most of us be to make Peter more committed, Thomas less skeptical, and Judas more trusting?

What would we have done in Jesus' place if we had a chance to get back at the Pharisees? Would we be able to let go of our anger toward them the way Jesus did and continue with a productive and peaceful life? Or would we hang on to our anger and give in to the "Don Corleone instinct" by getting even?

Certainly, I find it hard to let go. I find it almost impossible to forgive my enemies, especially when I'm still feeling the sting of their insults. I don't even know any good psychological tricks that make it any easier to let go.

The only thing that works for me is prayer. I start praying where I am. I don't say anything grandiose like "Oh, Lord, I place all the universe in your hands, and I am your obedient servant." I never say anything like that because it isn't true. In fact just the opposite is true. I want all the universe in *my* hands. I don't want to let go of anything.

So instead of trying to impress God (and myself), I ask God for the grace to forgive. "Just help me do it a little bit, Lord." I ask for the ability to let go of all the thoughts that trouble me. I ask for the grace to put these people, these past sins, or these dumb mistakes in his hands so I can get them out of my mind.

Prayer works for me. Letting go is something that seems beyond my power at times, and prayer is always the best method for dealing with anything beyond our power. Whenever I pray for a spiritual favor that will help me love better, I get an answer.

Love is the greatest law. If we ask for the grace to fulfill that law, God won't refuse. When we let go, we always love better.

11

LOVING DAY BY DAY

By this time no one needs to tell us that love is the foundation and the heart of Christian living. We all know this, and for the most part we all strive to love.

I'm often struck by couples who have been married forty, fifty, and sixty years. I wonder about the kinds of problems they have lived through and yet continue to love and the struggles they have endured to maintain love over such a long period of time.

I know a teacher who has been teaching first grade for forty years. It's impressive to see a young, healthy man or woman come into a classroom of first-graders and be enthusiastic, loving, and motivated. But for a woman in her sixties, feeling the normal aches and pains, shifting moods, and relationship problems of that stage of life and no longer enamored by the newness of her job, to come into the classroom each day smiling and enthusiastic with a heart full of love for those children approaches the heroic.

I'm impressed with the public-health nurse who has been visiting homes day in and day out for over twenty years, yet meets each patient as if every day were her first day on the job. She talks to each family member with the same sensitive, warm smiling face that was hers over twenty years ago.

We all know that love is the goal of Christian living. But we have to keep in mind that love is not just something we feel at the beginning of a marriage or career. For a Christian, love is something we must have today, carefully maintain, and continue to express every day of our lives.

Many people are good at loving in the first stages of a marriage, when everything is new and romantic and emotionally charged. Others have no trouble showing warmth, enthusiasm, and love in the first year or two of a career. But we have to make sure that not only the beginning stages of our marriage or career but also the middle and final stages are filled with love.

We don't have to be as enthusiastic in our fifties as we were in our twenties. Being a cheerleader is not necessarily loving. But regardless of our age, we need a heart within us that cares and reaches out to God and our fellow human beings.

This might seem to be a superhuman task. To think that we can love every day of our lives, despite our aches and pains and the problems that press upon our families, is a bit presumptuous. There is just too much going on for us to think that we could be loving despite all the challenges.

We have to pray for a lasting love. We have to pray for the grace and the perseverance to cope with our own feelings and the stress that comes our way. Not through our own efforts alone but through the free gift of God's grace will we continue to love day in and day out until the end of our lives.

The difference between the mature Christian and the immature Christian is that the mature person realizes just how dependent upon God's grace we really are. Maintaining a loving, giving heart for a lifetime demands all the grace we can get. If we think we can do it by ourselves, we are merely massaging our egos.

We have only to look at Saint Augustine to see the power that grace can have in our lives. Not only did he have trouble believing, he was a driven, restless man with very little peace of mind. Yet after his conversion he had a deep faith and an undisturbed peace. While he was dying, the Vandals were attacking the gates of his city; but through all this pain and turmoil Augustine remained faithful, peaceful, and loving.

God's grace can make dramatic transformations. It can turn any one of us, even the most self-centered, into a great Christian lover. Pray for the grace to love, for love is the greatest law. God will surely not turn away if we ask for the grace to fulfill his greatest law.

12

TRUSTING IN GOD

A middle-aged man was describing a nervous problem he had as a young teen when he felt everything he did was a sin. Even the thoughts that flashed through his mind seemed like sins. Nothing he did helped. Nothing his confessors said relieved the feeling of guilt.The solution came only when he placed his life in God's hands. Trusting himself to God's mercy rather than his own brought him complete relief from his scruples.

Several years later this man found himself in college. As he studied about freedom and personality, he began to think that God was less and less in control of things. His trust in God foundered, and his previous nervous troubles returned. They persisted for years, and only through a combination of psychotherapy and spiritual direction did he finally regain a solid equilibrium through a renewed trust in God.

Trust in God is not something we need momentarily or even for a number of years. Trust in God is something we need constantly throughout our lives.

Society will always have its trends. There are times when trusting in God is the norm for everyone, from the pope to the peasant. At other times freedom, "rugged individualism," and personal power are in vogue.

Sometimes we are insensitive to the subtle changes in thought and belief in society. We may not perceive the trend toward human beings trusting themselves totally and forgetting about God. Because we don't see what is happening, it is easy to go along with the crowd without realizing what we are doing. Christians can't get caught up in every trend.

Trust in the Father was a hallmark of Jesus' ministry. Trust wasn't something that Jesus developed the night before the crucifixion. Jesus trusted the Father each day. He trusted that as long as he did what the

Father willed, everything would work out. It might not work out as quickly or in the same manner that we humans wish, but it would work out.

Jesus' trust in the Father ran counter to some of the thinking in vogue in his day. Some of his followers wanted Jesus to take a more forceful stand against the power structure and assert the reign of God. But Jesus refused to get caught up in trends and fads. He trusted in God instead.

The saints throughout the centuries lived through all kinds of trends. Some saints lived in tranquil environments where everyone seemed to trust in God. Theresa of Lisieux, "the Little Flower," trusted deeply in God, reflecting the trust of her family and community. But Francis of Assisi's neighbors thought he was a little eccentric for trusting so much in God. His family and friends thought he should put a little more trust in material things.

Regardless of whether their environment supported trust in God or worked against it, one of the common characteristics of the saints was their trust in God. All the saints worked hard at their apostolates, but they all trusted in God as well. They knew too that if they did their best, things would work out God's way. Even if they didn't know how things would work out, they were sure that God would be there. That was enough for them, and they trusted him.

Trust in the Father was at the heart of Jesus' life, and it was central in the lives of his most illustrious followers. Trust is not something that we can opt for. Trust is essential for the Christian. It is at the core of the Christian life. There is no other way for the Christian to live.

Karl Rahner, a popular theologian at the time of the Vatican Council, wrote, "To lead a Christian life is to place one's whole being into the hands of God as confidently as a child takes the guiding hand of [his or her] father."

Trust never goes out of style. Philosophies, trends, and fads may come and go. But for the committed Christian the only way to make this walk through life successfully is with trust in God.

13

CHOOSING COMMUNITY

In the Old West, no matter how much they may have liked the wide-open spaces, families tended to build their homes close enough to one another for protection. Despite their distance from one another, these families felt secure in knowing that their neighbors could come to their aid.

There is strength in numbers and a certain amount of security in banding together. Throughout history we have seen how movements such as the labor movement and the civil rights movement have succeeded when people with a common cause stand together.

When the people of God stand together for security, strength, or just to fulfill a deep social need for belonging, we call this community. When this community comes together to worship, it is fulfilling its deepest yearnings.

Coming together with a group to worship God strengthens the faith of everyone in the group. Just as we were not meant to live alone, we were not meant to worship God by ourselves. While individual prayer has value, there is a time to get together with other like-minded people for worship.

I once worked at a busy agency that served the poor of the city. Like all the social workers there, I had a large caseload of clients to see each week. One day as I was on my way to visit some of the families on my list, a supervisor stopped me and told me to attend a meeting. I replied that I would be glad to attend but I had quite a few families to see that afternoon. My supervisor revealed her wisdom when she said, "You need that meeting because getting together with the other social workers will be a good support for you."

In the same way, getting together with other Christians to worship

God is a good support for all of us. No matter how many things we need to do, this contact with other Christians reminds us of the very essence of our lives. Even though we are distracted by many duties and people, gathering with other Christians to worship and socialize helps us to refresh and rebuild ourselves.

Community is never easy. There are always some insincere, egotistical, or unreliable people in community. Yet we have to be careful not to judge the many by the few. Living in community means that we have to overlook the shortcomings of the few for the good of the whole group.

Community is not a clique, nor is it a social club. It takes all kinds of people to make a Christian community, and imitating Jesus' love means accepting the differences and shortcomings in one another without being self-righteous. People can and do grow through their relationships with the Christian community.

Sometimes community asks us to do things we don't want to do. Sometimes because of community, we have to smile when we don't want to smile and talk when we feel like remaining silent. This too is an important part of community.

The letters of Saint Paul and Saint Peter constantly urge community members to show hospitality to one another. In his first epistle, Peter urges the brethren not only to show hospitality but also to be good sports about it and stop grumbling.

Saint Thomas More was widely known for his hospitality. He often entertained guests, and the poor were frequently invited. Throughout history, convents and monasteries have been famous for their willingness to show hospitality to travelers.

The community literally pulls us out of ourselves. To live in community, we have to stop thinking of ourselves, at least part of the time. I have heard parents say that their children have made them reach heights of self-forgetfulness they never would have imagined reaching on their own. Community can do the same thing for us.

Community requires sacrifices. Yet these sacrifices are slight compared to what we can receive from community. It is no wonder that people choose being together over being alone. Christians must make that same choice.

14

HAVING COURAGE

One of the virtues we often forget when we think of the spiritual life and our relationship with God is courage. Too often we associate courage with battlefield heroics, forgetting that it is a necessary part of everyday life, even the spiritual life.

Archbishop Oscar Romero of San Salvador felt a great compassion for the poor people of his country. He began doing everything he could to bring about justice for the poor and suffering of El Salvador. He used not only the pulpit but all the resources at his command — letters, newspaper articles, and radio — to let everyone know about the sufferings of the poor.

Some government leaders, angered by Archbishop Romero's emphasis on the suffering of the poor, threatened him with violence. He was frightened; but this is precisely what courage is — the ability to do what we know must be done even though we may not feel like doing it.

Despite his fear, Archbishop Romero continued his crusade for the poor and suffering people. Truly, his confidence in God and his love for his people gave him the courage to go on. Then on March 24, 1980, Archbishop Romero was shot and killed while celebrating Mass.

Archbishop Romero's story is a dramatic example of courage that shows how one man conquered fear and took his faith and love to the ultimate limit. You and I may never have the opportunity to stand up and defend all the poor and suffering people of our nation. We may never have to confront great masses of political and social opposition. Yet we need courage in our daily lives as surely as Archbishop Romero needed courage in his life.

At times we find it hard to pray because we don't have a good feeling or even any positive images of God. At these times our words seem to be floating out and fading into empty space rather than falling upon the ears of a loving God. At times like this our faith needs to be bolstered by our courage. And it is courage that enables us to continue to pray until the good feelings return.

There will be times in our lives when we will not feel like being patient with our children or affectionate toward our spouses. There will be times when we feel like throwing a tantrum and demanding our rights. At times like this we will need to reach for the courage to stand firm, to be loving and patient until the positive feelings return.

We'll need courage to reach out to others the way Jesus did. It took great courage for Jesus to continue to preach and heal when at times he obviously received very little in return. There must have been times when he even felt people were taking advantage of him and not hearing his basic message.

It takes courage to continue to be loving to the people we work with, even though at times they may seem to be out for themselves. It takes courage to do works of charity — whether in personal relationships with friends or through societies like St. Vincent de Paul or a parish soup kitchen. The courage consists not only of getting up and doing things for others but in persevering when we seem to be getting very little in return.

We are blessed when our prayers and our service spring spontaneously from our hearts, when we feel deeply satisfied by our work and moved to do it. But during those times when enthusiasm and spontaneity abandon us, we need to pray for God's grace so that we may have the courage to do what we know we should do.

15

KNOWING YOURSELF

What are our strengths and weaknesses? What do we like to do? How do we get along with others and in what ways do we serve best? What place does God have in our lives?

Answering these questions and others will help us understand a little better just exactly who we are. A little self-knowledge is the first step to serving others.

If we don't have a good idea of who we are, we will run into trouble in all areas of life. A woman who doesn't know she has a bad heart will be in a lot of trouble if she tries to run a twenty-six-mile marathon. The married man who doesn't recognize his own controlling nature is in for trouble. Helpful Christians will encounter trouble if they remain unaware of how dependent in many ways they are upon the people they help. It goes on and on. Wisdom means knowing ourselves.

There isn't any trick to knowing ourselves, although it takes a certain amount of humility and open-mindedness. Then it takes a desire to let things be. We are never going to know ourselves completely. That is why we ultimately depend on God, who reads our hearts, our minds, and our unconscious.

It's important to remember that there is nothing wrong with the way we are. Our preconceptions about what we should be often make us ashamed of what we are. We may differ from one another drastically, but God has made our very differences part of his plan.

G.K. Chesterton described a dinner at which Saint Thomas Aquinas and King Louis IX of France, better known as Saint Louis, were present. Saint Thomas was a physically large man. Although always friendly, courteous, and kind, he was a quiet, often preoccupied intellectual. On the other hand, Saint Louis was a king, a man of action, well versed in the martial arts. The two men had entirely different personalities: the quiet, passive saint and the active, outgoing, aggressive saint. Most of us fall somewhere in between these two extremes. But we have to find out roughly who we are and then take that and begin moving toward God.

No particular personality type is more suited to sainthood than another. In spite of our sins, we are well suited to sainthood just as we are now. But the first thing we have to do is find out who we are so that we can use our unique personalities for service. Straining and pushing ourselves to be other than what we are will make us neither happy nor holy.

No doubt Saint Thomas would have been miserable as a king, and Saint Louis would have been bored as a monk. Fortunately, these two men found such complete ways to express their personalities that they became saints. We need to learn about ourselves so that we can also express ourselves as the saints did.

When a businessman I knew felt that God was calling him to serve somewhere other than in business, he didn't rush to quit his job. He knew that learning who he was and where he could best serve would be a delicate task. After he recognized the desire to do some other kind of work, he prayed, trusting that the Lord would let him know if he wanted him to serve elsewhere.

His patience paid off. About a month after he began praying for guidance to know himself, a friend asked if he knew someone interested in working as a volunteer coordinator for the local hospital. The job description and salary fit his needs, and he found a new place to express himself as a Christian.

Prayer helps us face who we are and what we can do. We cannot know ourselves completely through our own efforts. We have to rely on God to give us glimpses of new self-knowledge from time to time. In the meantime, we have to go on using ourselves to the best of our ability. Knowing who we are is important, but it is also a lifetime job.

16

FACING CHANGE

In the 1940s a college professor wrote that he couldn't predict how his students would turn out because society was changing so fast. I had to chuckle when I read that. If he thought things were changing fast in the forties, he should see the changes in the eighties and nineties.

Nevertheless, people in every age have been aware of things changing around them. The apostles must have thought the earth was shifting under their feet after the Resurrection. The early Christians must have thought their world had changed forever when they had to go underground to worship. In the sixties every Catholic felt the shock waves of change from Vatican II. Some resisted the changes; others rushed them, forgetting why they were changing.

Change is part of life. Since the advent of computers, how many people have seen their jobs change? How many close relationships have changed because a friend married, divorced, or moved away? Every time we look our children are changing. Whether we like it or not, our bodies are constantly in the process of change. The very planet that sustains us is changing.

Change is obviously part of God's plan, or he would have frozen Adam and Eve in the Garden and never allowed them to make choices. If God didn't want things to change, he wouldn't have given us free will.

Christians have to live with change as a way of life, not hide from it or always be struggling to prevent it. Christians accept change with hope and faith, then jump into the change with both feet and try to make it a growing experience rather than a tension-filled regression. Mature Christians do not have to be dragged into the future kicking, screaming, and clinging for dear life to the past. They walk boldly and hopefully into the future.

Even when the change is not to our liking, psychological maturity and Christian courtesy dictate that we be good sports about it, not grumbling or trying to find fault with the change to prove a point. The Christian who has faith in God's plan and hope in God's providence will find it easier to be a good sport about change.

People often resist change because they are afraid that things will not change for the better. So they fear a new supervisor. They worry about the new neighbors. They don't want major changes in the economy or in their parish. They secretly long for the "good old days."

We need to be wise enough to plan for the future, but we do not need to worry about it. In order to be open to love and relatively at peace, Christians must not only have faith in God's plan for a changing world, they also need to have hope in God's constant presence and care for us as we change.

When we cling to the past for its own sake and resist change, we place our trust in institutions and procedures rather than in God. We have a misplaced emphasis when we believe that it is solely the institution that does good instead of God's grace working through the institution.

A Christian woman was being teased by some people at work: "How can you put your faith in a Church that is at times so materialistic and has had sinners — like Augustine — for theologians?"

"I don't put my ultimate faith in institutions," she said. "My faith is in Jesus. And by the way, Augustine would be the first one to tell you he was a sinner and that only by putting his faith in Jesus was he able to do anything good."

When our faith is in Jesus, change is less threatening. Some changes are good; others are not so good. But whatever happens, Jesus is with us. Jesus lives in us and in the Church, giving us the grace to grow with the change.

A bishop I know always said that no matter what happened there would always be Jesus.

We don't know what is coming tomorrow. But what difference does it make? Jesus will be there. Regardless of the changes that lie ahead, "What can separate us from the love of Jesus Christ?"

17

SEEKING GRACE

The words of Saint Ignatius, "Your love and your grace are enough for me," are dramatic words — the words of a saint. There is so much in life that we need. We can be practical and logical. We can come up with a long list of needs and justify every one of them on moral grounds. We can even show how these needs are necessary for spiritual growth.

But when we come down to it, how many of us can truly say that God's grace is enough for us? If God granted us one wish, would we say, "I wish for your grace"? Or would we ask for our present burning need?

If I were ill, I would be tempted to ask for health. If I were about to lose my home through foreclosure, I'd probably ask for a mortgage payment. But even beyond that, should we ask for world peace or relief from hunger — or for God's grace?

It's a dilemma for our limited minds. Fortunately, these are theoretical questions because the Lord is sure to understand any sincere request intended to do good.

But God's grace implies the fullness of life. With his grace our faith would be fuller, more complete. Consequently, our understanding would be clearer. With grace we would see God as he is rather than as we want him to be. We would view world problems and the suffering of our brothers and sisters with the eyes of faith. We might even have the courage to make a response to what we see.

God's grace would resolve many of our own problems. Perhaps if God gave us the grace to believe more fully in him, we wouldn't be so pessimistic about the future or so gloomy after listening to the news. In many instances God's grace may even lessen our anxiety.

God's grace doesn't just change us intellectually; it can change us emotionally as well. Grace can make us different people, just as it changed the apostles from cringing, frightened men to bold, undaunted witnesses. Grace changed Thomas Merton from a man immersed in worldly concerns to a monk bent on acquiring a relationship with God. Grace changed Dorothy Day into a woman with burning zeal for the poor.

Grace can change us from lukewarm people to committed Christians with hearts full of love. Grace can change us from irritated, restless people to men and women of peace. Grace can change us from materialistic people to people who see what is really important in life.

To prepare ourselves for grace we have to remove all the obstacles. We have to be men and women of goodwill, and we have to do what we can to make ourselves healthy in mind and body.

A retired man prayed for the grace to spend his remaining years in a productive and loving way. But despite his prayers he felt he was wasting time sleeping late, watching TV, and doing nothing that he considered productive.

Then one day he spoke with a Sister who worked as a pastoral counselor in his parish. Recognizing immediately that the man was depressed, she suggested that he see his doctor. The doctor prescribed medication, and the Sister provided insight and encouragement.

In about a month the man started to feel better. The barricade was removed, and the grace he had been praying for began to flow. First he visited a few friends in the hospital. Then he joined the prison ministry in his parish. Soon he was involved and productive.

Sometimes we have to take a close look at our lives to see if there is any obstacle to grace. Maybe it is a lingering prejudice that we can't get rid of. Or it can be a stubborn way of doing things that we refuse to change. We are never too old to change. Let's not block God's grace.

Finally, since God's grace is a gift, something we can never earn, we need to pray for it. We need to ask that it be given to us. It is a free gift.

We don't capture grace. We merely receive it from a God who loves us and wishes to share himself with us. So let us remove all obstacles, pray for the gift, and then be open to receive it. God's grace is enough for us.

18

ACCEPTING DISAPPOINTMENT

"I called on a friend because I needed a job," the man was saying. "I had never asked him for anything before, but I felt confident that he would help, especially when he saw that I had lost my job.

"But it didn't turn out the way I thought it would. He said he couldn't help me because things were slow. He expected me to understand his problem. I was more than a little disappointed."

When we are disappointed, we become angry. We wonder how a trusted friend, a spouse, or a child could do this to us. We feel a righteous indignation. We are sure that God is on our side and that he too is angry at those who have disappointed us. Sometimes disappointment can make us feel like whipped pups, slinking off into a corner to lick our wounds. These are the times when we feel sorry for ourselves.

But whether we feel self-righteous or whipped, disappointment makes us feel negative. Yet as bad as we feel when it happens, disappointment is part of life. We can't avoid it. In fact we can count on being disappointed at some time or another.

Even Jesus wasn't exempt from disappointment. His mission was noble; he had come to redeem people. Yet the powerful people of his time worked against him, never supporting him or helping him get his message across. If this wasn't bad enough, his twelve most trusted friends, his companions of three years, didn't stand by him in the end but ran away and hid.

Jesus in his humanness truly felt the sting of disappointment. But his reaction to disappointment is instructive. He never complained. He never felt self-righteous. He never got so depressed over his disappointments that he couldn't continue. Jesus accepted the reality of human relationships. He understood that people will be loving and supportive sometimes and at other times they will disappoint us. He accepted the fact that people do not always act ideally or perfectly — even though we want them to.

When dealing with people, we need to take the same realistic approach that Jesus did. We shouldn't be pessimists and say that since all people are the same we can't trust anyone. On the other hand, an overly romantic idealism only sets us up for disappointment. We need to remember the goodness and loyalty of others while not being surprised or devastated when they act otherwise.

Louis Braille had a desire to read, despite the fact that a childhood infection had left him blind. In the early part of the nineteenth century, however, there was no method to help him accomplish this. When he was twelve, Louis started thinking about some way to enable blind people to read. He experimented with a pin and paper; but instead of supporting and encouraging him, some of his friends began to laugh at him for his foolish idea. But Louis never gave up. Using all his free time for three years, he developed the alphabet for the blind that was named after him.

Had Louis Braille felt self-righteous indignation after being disappointed by his friends, he might have spent his time getting even rather than inventing an alphabet. If he had felt put down and embarrassed, he might have wasted his time in depression rather than creativity. Only a realistic appraisal of others can keep us from being thrown off track when we are disappointed.

We could take this one step further and say that everyone in our lives will disappoint us to some extent. We have come to expect impeccable loyalty from our family and friends. We crave that perfect relationship, that perfect security. Sometimes we are to blame for our own disappointment; we just expect too much from others.

Perfect relationships are impossible. The only person who will never disappoint us is God. Accepting the limitations of our human relationships may be what we need to truly appreciate the infinite wealth we have in our relationship with God.

19

PRAYING YOUR ANGER

Many people are angry today and don't even know it. They are so angry they can't get along with family members. They are so angry they can't enjoy Christian community. They are so angry they can't even pray properly.

They deny that they are angry. "I'm not angry," they say. "I never shout, yell, or insult anyone." But their anger seeps out slowly and subtly. They criticize others. They always see the negative side of people and institutions. They are cynical, often preferring to be alone rather than be close to someone who might annoy them. They never voice it, but hundreds of little things disgust them.

They usually can't figure out what is going on with themselves. They are restless. They toss and turn and never feel as though they quite fit in. At times they feel like psychological and spiritual misfits.

From time to time we all fit this category, since we all get angry. Because many of us feel that anger is unworthy of Christians, we refrain from acting angrily (which is good); but unfortunately, we then carry it one step further and try to refrain from *feeling* anger.

It is impossible to shut off our feelings. If we do, our anger will come out in other ways, such as cynicism, disgust, or withdrawal. Jesus was right when he advised us to reconcile with one another before we offer our gift at the altar. Repressed anger will distract us, consume us, and even disorient our thinking. The more we take care of our anger, the better we are able to pray.

It is true that acting out anger in ways that are destructive and hurtful to others is immature and antisocial. However, we Christians should be honest enough and humble enough to admit when we are angry and, if possible, discover why we are angry. If we can do this without acting on our anger, then we are on the road to not only changing our feelings but also growing with them.

A spiritual exercise that used to be quite popular — but which no longer seems to be in vogue — is the daily examination of conscience. This exercise was a good opportunity to check up on ourselves and be honest with our feelings. Perhaps it would be beneficial if we stopped more often in our busy lives to take such a look inside.

A daily examination of conscience might reveal that we are cynical, disgusted, or annoyed. Then if we look at the circumstances surrounding our anger, we might understand the root of it. Once we do this, we are in a good position to do something about our anger. In psychotherapy, patients are encouraged to talk about their anger and to keep talking until they see things differently, feel differently, or discover a way to resolve the anger. It's a tried-and-true method that works.

For Christians who have honestly come to the conclusion that they are angry, even though they aren't acting angrily, the next step is to talk to God about the anger. That's right; pray your anger. Tell God how disgusted you are. Describe to God how miserable you feel. Don't be afraid to tell him that right now you feel the whole world is wrong and you are right. Let God know, although he knows already, how your anger is eating you up and dragging you down.

Then tell God what you really want. Plead for his love and grace so the energy that now feeds the anger will be transformed into love and peace. Tell him how you would really like to feel toward others. Maybe you would like to be more committed to your ideals and less focused on the petty things that get you so disgusted. Perhaps you would like to be man enough or woman enough to talk to someone about your anger instead of just stewing over it.

Whatever it is, turn your anger and your desire into prayer. Pray your feelings. Jeremiah, the great Old Testament prophet, poured his heart out to God. When he was imprisoned for speaking the word of the Lord, Jeremiah told God that he would never speak God's word again. Then he said he felt a burning desire to keep going on.

Our feelings are natural. God created us with the ability to feel. We shouldn't act on all our feelings, but we can't help feeling them. So tell God what you feel and what you need. He made our feelings. He is the one who truly understands them.

20

DEALING WITH GUILT

"I'm sorry."
"It was my fault"
"I feel terrible"
"I shouldn't have."

Statements such as these constantly tumble from the lips of those who often feel guilty. They are nice, well-meaning, responsible people; but they see everything that goes wrong as their fault.

These are the folks who never think they do a good enough job, whether they are raising kids, working at their jobs, or volunteering at church. Consequently, they do not enjoy what they do. They are always pushing and striving to do better and better. They think someone is always about to call them on the carpet and scold them.

There are times when we should feel guilty. If we lie, cheat, steal, or fail to help someone in need, the guilt we feel is justified. Nevertheless, guilt should not paralyze us or depress us so much that we cannot function. If you feel overwhelmed by guilt, whether unjustified or justified, think and pray about the following.

First, God created you to be happy — not necessarily wealthy and powerful, but peaceful, content, and secure. While a sense of responsibility is a virtue, being guilt ridden is not. When we are parenting, working, or volunteering, God expects us to be responsible; but he also wants us to enjoy our work, to find peace in it, and to leave the results to him.

Many people persevere in parenting and service work for years because they enjoy the work. They do not drive themselves out of guilt or a need to prove something by accomplishing unrealistic goals. Guilt forces us to drive ourselves hard because we think we can never do anything right.

Second, let your guilt feelings work for you. They don't always have to be neurotic hangovers from the past. They can be signals that change is needed. You may feel some guilt because of what you said about a coworker or because of the bad example you set for your children by drinking or lying. Guilt in instances like this may rob you of some peace, but it can also be the road back to peace.

Admit your fault, first of all to yourself then to anyone else who may be involved. Next, make an attempt to rectify what you have done, if possible, or resolve not to do it again.

It is important also to be understanding and patient with ourselves. We cannot always stop destructive or sinful behavior just because we want to. Sometimes certain habits need to be broken before the sin can stop. In the process of breaking these habits, we do not have to berate ourselves for our lack of perfect behavior. Let the feeling of guilt be a gentle reminder that sometimes change is a process we need to work at steadily.

Saint Augustine emphasized that the Good Samaritan in the parable brought the wounded man to an inn and paid for the care necessary for his recuperation. His point was that healing does not come immediately; often it takes time and exacts a price. Guilt should work for us by reminding us to wait and pay the price. Guilt should never pull us down, destroy our motivation, and sap our zeal for change.

Finally, living in God's love is the goal of a Christian life. Whenever we feel guilt, whether it is the feeling that nothing we do is good enough or the fear that we will never be able to kick a bad habit, we must remember that we do not save ourselves or make ourselves holy. God makes us holy.

The sacrament of reconciliation is one of the ways through which we can live in God's love. It is a tangible way to confront our shortcomings and experience God's love for us through the Church. This sacrament affords us the opportunity to deal with guilt. There is nothing more we can do than admit our faults, ask for forgiveness, and try to do better. After that, we have to trust in the mercy and love of God.

21

LIVING WITH ILLNESS

Everyone, at some time or other, has to cope with illness. Perhaps the healthiest of the very young may temporarily be relieved from this type of suffering; but by and large, most us must struggle with illness some time in our lives.

It may be the woman who is waiting for a report on her biopsy or the man who has had migraines for twenty years. It may be the person struggling with depression or the man or woman working every day with a bad back. Sometimes it is people and their families attempting to cope with cancer or Alzheimer's disease. We all have our own Achilles heel. Even some little children must struggle with leukemia or epilepsy.

Yet as we go about our daily lives in our neighborhoods and offices, we don't see the quiet invisible suffering all around us. All we see are people moving about, functioning, interacting. We don't see beneath the surface. We don't listen to the faint voice of pain.

Do we fail to perceive the suffering of others because we are superficial? Do we simply deny the unpleasant? Or are we constantly seeking more and more for ourselves and only seeing what others have that we should have?

Illness, like death, is part of life. It is a sign that we are mortal and limited. Just as we have to accept the fact that we will die before we can live fully, so too we have to accept the fact that we will encounter headaches, diseases, and surgeries in this life.

Recognizing illness in ourselves and our world can help us live as Christians are supposed to live and lead us to a greater trust in God. Many things in this life are beyond our control; some are even beyond the control of medical science. We have to place our hands in the hand of God the Father, or we will be either constantly frightened or always trying to control things. Either way makes a Christian life hard to lead.

It is easier to talk about illness when we are healthy. When we are ill, we must call on our faith and draw closer to God. Most Christians move closer to God in suffering. The message in the gospel is clear; Jesus often reached out to heal the illnesses of the people he met. We have every reason to believe he will do the same for us as long as we are willing to go along with God's plan rather than our own.

Why some people suffer and others don't is not a question for us to answer. Our job is not to unravel the mystery of suffering but to have faith enough to throw ourselves into the hands of God.

"I volunteered with hospice in my community," one woman said. "But before I could really get involved, I had to get my thinking straight. I had trouble reconciling illness and suffering with a loving God, but I had to believe that God loves all these suffering people. Trying to answer the question of why they suffer is like playing God. It takes faith to believe in him, despite the suffering of the innocent. With renewed faith I forged ahead.

"And when I came close to these suffering people, I saw many manifestations of God's love. The peace in some of these families, the courage, the love of neighbors, all made me aware of God's presence here. Of course this does not offset the suffering they go through, but I realized that somehow God was here and he was unexplainable."

When we accept illness as a part of life rather than trying to explain it away, we put it in its place. This allows us to deal with our own illnesses and the illnesses of others in a more realistic way. Christians are better able to reach out to others if they are not intimidated by suffering. We do not have to like it. In fact we should pray for our own healing and the healing of others.

Nevertheless, illness will always be with us. Living with it, while trying to relieve it, is what it means to work for the kingdom.

22

ACCEPTING DEATH

Thoughts of death bring back boyhood memories of serving at funeral Masses on cold winter mornings. The priest and altar boys were dressed in black, and large black candleholders were used at funeral Masses. The organ pumped out the "Dies Irae," a Latin hymn about the Day of Judgment, the day of wrath. The pews were filled with crying people. I thought that this death thing was really scary, and I was glad it was not going to happen to me — or so I thought at the age of twelve.

A common practice when I was in high school and Catholic college was to meditate on death. This was scary too. We were supposed to remind ourselves that we were going to die, a fact that is hard to believe when you (and even your parents) are young and healthy and you are in love.

I was glad when this practice was replaced by the modern emphasis of Vatican II. In my young adulthood we focused on community, social justice, and self-fulfillment. It was a welcome break from death issues.

Then a funny thing happened in middle age. I found myself worrying more. I was visiting doctors more and enjoying it less. I worried about diet and exercise. I worried about every little change in my health. I was especially preoccupied with my heart.

I finally found that to be free of the ultimate fear that haunts us all and stifles many of us, I had to confront that old friend I first met at those funeral Masses as a boy. No one likes to think of death. But death is part of life, and we can't enjoy all of life until we accept all of life, including death.

The greatest event in all of Christianity was the Resurrection of Jesus. By this single act Jesus overcame death once and for all and made it possible for all who believe in him never to fear death again. But it takes a great deal of faith and constant reminding to keep death in its place.

In my years as a social worker in hospitals, hospice, and family practice, I have seen many people die. And many of these people have approached their terminal illnesses and ultimate deaths with serenity and peace. People not known previously for their great faith or their ability to let go have somehow found a way of relaxing in the face of death. It is something I hope I will be able to do when the time comes.

It is somehow comforting to know that it is possible, even in our materialistic world, for people to ultimately let go and trust God. Once we can put the ultimate fear in its place, all other fears fall into line and our freedom is multiplied.

I recently read the story of Janet Manternach Ripple, who died in 1982. She lived in Illinois with her husband, a judge, and their two children. Janet worked at a local college, had many friends, and enjoyed parties.

Then she was stricken with cancer. She fought it for ten years, and at times it looked as if she would win. But finally the doctors told her she had only a few months to live. She became sad and frightened of dying. She couldn't rest. Then a priest friend helped her find ways to pray. Listening to religious music as she lay in bed helped her to rest and grow in faith.

As her faith grew deeper, the pain grew stronger. She felt sad at the thought of leaving her children; like any parent she wanted to see them grow up. But even this natural longing was turned into a moment of faith for her. It was a chance to trust God to care for them.

Janet's faith helped her through this trying time. It helped her accept death and enabled her to let go. People were amazed and attracted by this woman who had so much by middle-class standards and yet was able to let go of it all so peacefully because of her faith.

Death is always with us. Even when we don't see it or hear about it, it is there. Most of us bury the thought of death. Of course we don't have to go to the other extreme and think about death all day long, but we need to remind ourselves that we have nothing to fear. Jesus conquered death for us. We can trust him.

23

KEEPING THE MYSTERY

In my pre-Vatican II college days we would resort to an old expression whenever we could not explain something about the Church or God. We'd say, "It's a mystery." Sometimes our professors would use the phrase to put an end to incessant questions by students. But everybody was familiar with the phrase, and we all knew what it meant. "I don't know how to explain this any further, but God knows."

The phrase was used so often it took on a social meaning. If you wondered why a certain girl didn't like you, a comforting friend would tell you, "It's a mystery." It became our favorite way to describe anything we could not understand, from people of the opposite sex to Russian novels.

But as the years went by, we gradually lost our sense of mystery. We learned a little bit more about Scripture, philosophy, and psychology; and we couldn't stop. We wanted to know everything. If somebody tried to tell us that something was a mystery, we'd cry, "Foul!" We even wanted to know how the mystery worked.

The same lack of a sense of mystery continues today. We want to know why we can't relate to certain people. We want to know why we fear, worry, and get depressed. We want to know why our children can't read, obey, or achieve. This need to know everything is so great that even the bookracks in supermarkets and drugstores offer answers to such ultimate questions as why women love, why men respond, why we fail or overeat, and what happens when we die.

We want all the answers. We will leave no stone unturned. Mystery is out; knowledge is in. We even want to know how God works. We want to analyze his personality and find out what makes him tick. We want to explain away once and for all the mysteries that have perplexed human beings since the dawn of time.

In a recent book, a Catholic theologian tried to explain why bad things happen in a world created by an all-loving God. The explanation was nice, but needless to say it didn't clear up the greatest mystery of all time. There's nothing wrong with the book. But there is something wrong with people expecting a book to clear up the mystery.

We have to let God be God. By nature God is an incomprehensible Being. There is no way I can explain him. If I can, then I'm talking about something other than God. Since he is God, he doesn't need to be justified. I don't know why bad things happen in a world created by a loving God. But I do know that God does not need me to plead his case and make excuses for him.

God is a mystery, and the way he works is a mystery. I can't understand him completely or the way he works, but what I know of him is enough for me. He's all loving. He's forgiving. He made me and my world. He promised to be with me always. He asked me to trust him and walk with him. That's all we need to know. That says a lot.

Of course we can study about God and try to know him better. But we always have to keep in mind that no matter how much we study and learn, God will always escape our understanding. This shouldn't frustrate us. We need to accept that.

Karl Rahner, one of the leading theologians at the time of Vatican II, was involved in a great deal of scholarly work, yet he was always quick to point out that God is "incomprehensible." That's what makes God God.

Mystery is no longer an excuse to end a conversation for which we have no answers. Mystery is a reality for those who have faith.

Albert Einstein said, "My religion consists of a humble admiration of the illimitable superior spirit who reveals himself in the slight details we are able to perceive with our frail and feeble mind."

What we know about God is only a small fraction compared to what we do not know about him. Because he is so great, we can take a great deal of comfort in a God who is a mystery.

24

SEIZING THE MOMENT

He's described in all four gospels as the man who buried Jesus. The gospel writers call him a holy and distinguished member of the Sanhedrin who wasn't part of the plan to execute Jesus.

We don't know much more about Joseph of Arimathea than that. But I've always pictured him as a bureaucrat, part of the political-legal system of his time, a member of the establishment. He wasn't a poor fisherman like Peter. He wasn't a rebel or an outcast. He moved in well-established orthodox circles, and he was wealthy. He had his society's stamp of approval. The lives of most saints run counter to society; Joseph of Arimathea's life seems to have run right along with society.

Jesus calls all of us to do different things at different times. He asked the rich young man who wanted to be perfect to sell everything he had and come follow him. He asked Zachaeus to give up half of what he had. But as far as we know, Jesus didn't ask Joseph of Arimathea to give up anything.

Yet Joseph was a disciple of Jesus. He was waiting for the reign of God; he just wasn't too public about it. John called him a "secret" disciple. Can you imagine what it must have been like being both a rich, respected member of the establishment and a secret disciple of Jesus? Joseph must have had to bite his tongue at times when he was with those who were against Jesus.

Joseph must have been torn on many occasions. Should he or should he not declare himself? Was it the right time to stand up for Jesus? It must have been a stressful existence.

How often do we find ourselves in the same spot? We have a good job, enjoy a certain social position, have the "right" friends, and at the same time are disciples of Jesus. Sometimes we might even act like secret disciples, since no one can tell what we believe. Our true convictions are a blur because we try to please so many people.

We go along with people who place the highest value on acquiring money because we don't want to sound "corny." When we are with people who are prejudiced or slander other individuals, we let it slide because we don't want to be "self-righteous." We never talk about the Christian way because we don't want to be "fanatics."

Joseph of Arimathea must have often found himself in similar circumstances. He must have struggled with the same little daily choices we face. Perhaps on occasion he even rationalized his behavior just as we do: "It's better that I don't speak up. I can do more good for the organization from the inside as a respected member."

But when the chips were on the table, Joseph of Arimathea made his move with courage and drama. The end had come. Jesus was dead. The apostles were gone. There was anger in the streets and in the high places. If there was ever a time for a bureaucrat to "lie low," it was now.

So at last the secret disciple went public. Deep down he must have thought, *Enough is enough; now is the time to act.* Mark says that he "courageously went to Pilate and asked for the body of Jesus." This was the body that no one seemed to want.

When he asked Pilate for that body, there was no turning back. When he went out to Golgotha to take that body down from the cross, the whole world knew where Joseph of Arimathea stood. He stood squarely on the side of Jesus. The secret disciple made as bold and daring a declaration of faith as any follower of Jesus.

When the right time comes for you and me to make our move, will we have the grace to do it with the same courage and daring? Most likely it will not come in the form of such high drama. Most likely it will involve several small opportunities to show love. Perhaps it will be a chance to say something positive about a person no one else likes. Maybe it will be an opportunity to opt for a loving choice in the midst of anger. Maybe we will stoop to help a child and no one will know. But then again, high drama isn't always necessary.

Joseph of Arimathea was like us in many ways. His greatness came because he seized his moment. We must watch and pray so that we too can seize our moment.

25

DOING GOD'S WILL

Jesus was addressing a crowd when his mother came to speak with him. Someone interrupted Jesus to tell him that his mother was outside, and he made a remarkable statement.

"Who is my mother?" he asked. Then he went on to say, "Whoever does the will of my heavenly Father is brother and sister and mother to me."

Closeness to Jesus is guaranteed to us if we do the will of the Father. Jesus set the example for us. His whole life was a quest to do the will of the Father. "I came down from heaven not to do my own will but the will of the one who sent me" (John 6:38).

How do we discover God's will? Most of us don't even know what we want, much less what God wants. Discovering God's will may sound like a terribly complicated process, but it isn't. God's will is simple and often obvious, at least in the broad picture. "For this is the will of my Father, that everyone who sees the Son and believes in him may have eternal life" (John 6:40).

First, God wants us to have faith. So instead of floundering around fretting about how mysterious and hidden God's will is, we can start with what we know he wants us to do: work on increasing and developing our faith. Next, God wants us to love one another. That is obvious from everything Jesus tells us and everything the Church has been telling us through the centuries.

So when we think of doing God's will, we don't have to search far afield. We don't have to look for exotic things to do or for special messages from the Lord. His will is clearly defined — faith and love.

This faith and love will help us find God's will in the specific details of our lives. Faith and love will lead us to work on strengthening our marriage relationship if we are married. With faith and love as our goal, we will also have a clearer view of relationships that are detrimental to doing God's will. If we strive to believe in God and love one another, we will be able to accept the sacrifices and pains of parenting.

If we continue in our fidelity to God's will in the obvious matters, the less obvious things in life will also begin to take on the stamp of his will. Saint Martin de Porres was a Dominican lay helper. He worked in the monastery barber shop, took care of supplies, and visited the sick. In other words he spent his days doing the little ordinary things that need to be done to keep life flowing day by day. In terms of our modern lifestyles, they would be equal to doing laundry, disciplining children, and driving through traffic.

Martin's mother thought he should be a little more ambitious and become a priest. Martin, however, wasn't interested in anything more than doing little things with enthusiasm and love for God. And when you do things with love and enthusiasm, the most menial task can take on new meaning.

God endowed Saint Martin de Porres with extraordinary spiritual gifts. People attributed miracles to his prayers, and he became famous for his holiness and his remarkable charity to the poor, the sick, slaves, and even animals. This humble saint's life is a good example for those of us who get a little too ambitious about God's will and miss the obvious.

If we pay attention to the will of God in the little details of our lives, we too will be pulled along to greater things. Catherine Marshall was an ordinary woman who took her faith and her marriage seriously. She relied on her faith to sustain her through the loss when her husband Peter Marshall, a minister, died.

Then she felt a desire to write. She took a gamble, quit her job, and spent a year writing. At first she met disappointment, but eventually she became an accomplished and popular Christian writer. If, like Catherine Marshall, we are able to persevere in faith, God will continue to let us know what the loving thing to do is in each situation. And when we continue to do the loving thing, we are holy and we are doing God's will.

If we make belief in Jesus and love of others our way of doing God's will, he will lead us in the subtle decisions of life. We will not have to look far to see his will if we are tuned to faith and love.

The greatest thing we can do in this world is God's will. And we start doing his will by believing in him and loving one another. After that God will show us the rest. He will also give us the courage to follow his will wherever it may lead.

26

GROWING ON THE PILGRIMAGE

Charlotte Towle, a social worker in the middle of this century, described three ways of viewing life. One way is to see it as a treadmill. The person who follows this model does the same thing day after day, makes no changes, and hopes that circumstances never demand that changes be made.

The second way is to see life as a saga. The person who stars in a saga lives on the edge with great drama. He or she may risk everything and find great wealth, fame, or heroism but is just as likely to risk everything and lose. Everything the saga star does is of epic proportions.

Then there is the lifestyle that is made to order for the Christian — the pilgrimage. Pilgrims are always on the move. They are always in pursuit of their goal. They search; they get lost; they find their way again. They constantly need to adapt to changes in their environment. They need to solve all kinds of problems along the way.

We need to be pilgrims, and we need to remind ourselves frequently that we are pilgrims. So often we get upset because another problem has arisen in the family, with the children, or in our work. We shouldn't view problems only as annoyances but merely as part of growing on the pilgrimage.

Christians, like pilgrims, do not arrive at their destinations in this world. We haven't finished our tasks when our children are through adolescence or when we have attained a certain position at work. New problems will always be there for us.

When a man and a woman first marry, they have to get to know and understand each other. If they have children, they have to adjust to parenting, with all its stages of development. The empty nest, retirement, and older stages of life all demand their own difficult adjustments.

If we don't approach life as pilgrims — growing, searching, adapting — the alternative is to stagnate. But in order to grow we have to stay open-minded. We have to be vigilant to the opportunities that come to us for growth. We have to plan for the future, but we also need to be open to the grace of the moment. A pilgrim has a destination but is always aware of new twists and turns in the journey.

Albert Schweitzer, the son of a Lutheran pastor, was a teacher with a secure future who gave piano and organ concerts. As a young man he became well known for a book he wrote about Jesus. But the poor and suffering people were always on his mind. He wanted to do something to help them.

In the true spirit of a pilgrim, Albert Schweitzer heard God's call. Feeling his concern for the poor to be an invitation to serve, he became a doctor and set up a hospital in the African jungle. There he and his wife, a nurse, worked with the sick and the poor for fifty-two years.

In his early life Schweitzer enjoyed some impressive accomplishments. If he had lacked the open mind and keen awareness of a pilgrim, he might have stopped looking for opportunities to grow. Had he considered his goals accomplished because he was giving concerts and writing books, he never would have heard his true call. He would have literally missed the opportunity of a lifetime.

We never know what God has in store for us. We never quite arrive. Pray and stay vigilant so that you can follow God's will for you. The stories of the saints and holy people are filled with sensitive men and women making changes in their lives in order to grow closer to God. Dorothy Day turned to the working poor. Ignatius Loyola started the Jesuits. Mother Teresa went from teaching school to serving the poorest of the poor.

Life is always changing. We are always growing. The changes in our lives need not be as dramatic as those in the saints' lives. But God may call us to move from the complacency of our well-ordered home to a more active role in trying to cope with our teenagers as they experience problems. He might ask us to help out in our parishes or communities by volunteering in ordinary ways. A change in our business or our job status may be a call for us to serve God in another place or in another way.

Our true home is in heaven. Until then we have to stay on the move, ever trying, ever attentive to God's subtle voice in our lives. The only thing that can stop us is the false belief that we have arrived, that this is our true home. That kind of attitude will lull us to sleep.

Pray. Be vigilant. Be a faithful pilgrim.